THE
DREAM
WORKBOOK

A Simple Guide to
Interpreting Your Dreams

STEVEN MADDOX
and GINNY MADDOX

TABLE OF CONTENTS

INTRODUCTION

Dreams are fantastic messengers that tell us more about ourselves than we can even imagine. Everyone has access to this dream world, and we are all given the ability to interpret our dreams. However, only a few have had the expertise and understanding to teach us how to interpret our dreams. Most of the dream resources out there are now more of a dictionary than a personal guide to interpreting our dreams.

The Dream Book lays out the framework for interpreting your own dreams. This workbook shows you how to apply the principles that are taught in The Dream Book. We can have dreams that wow us or even scare us, but how much would our lives change if we could understand our dreams and take the deep complexities we see and break them down into something meaningful and applicable to our lives?

Dreams are meant to be interpreted. I want to give you some tools and self-discovery opportunities to break out some dreams and learn how to properly apply them in your life. This workbook will follow some of the same principles and guidelines found in The Dream Book. However, you will see added components that will allow you to go deeper. At the end of the day, it's up to you in terms of how much you want to get out of this resource. I really want you to consider pursuing your dreams and dream interpretation as a vital component to understanding yourself and the context of your life. This isn't something that you can just check off and say that you did it. When you begin to understand your dreams, your life will literally change.

If you are just picking up this book for the first time and are unfamiliar with The Dream Book, I would encourage you to read that one first. It will give you the basic principles and framework for applying this dream workbook. If you are familiar with The Dream Book concepts, it is possible to proceed with this workbook, but I would definitely encourage you to read that one first. How can we go down this path of common understanding if we are unfamiliar with the concepts that are being presented?

If you get this, you will unlock one of the greatest resources of your life. The ability to know yourself at an unconscious level and to be able to receive direction, warning, and divine purpose at the essential moments of your life are so important. I couldn't be more excited for you to take the steps to become a master of your own dreams. Okay, Dreamers, let's unpack some dreams.

Who are you?

Before we can dive into the nitty gritty and symbolic nature of our dreams to find out what they mean, we need to have a frame of reference to work from. This is called our baseline. Also, before we can get into breaking down our dreams, we need to understand the dreamer. The dreamer, the one who produces these dreams, is you. If you are not understood, then your dreams will never be. So one of the first things we are going to do is take an assessment. This will help to find your baseline, so that you are able to use the known parts of you to help establish your dream life and language.

What most people do is start talking about their dreams and forget that they are tied to someone specifically. In The Dream Book, I discussed in great detail how your dreams are inherently tied to you. You can't separate yourself from your dreams because they are a part of you, an extension of you. You may be inclined to just skip ahead and try to discover the symbolic meanings that have been chasing you around for the last decade. However, some things need to be progressive, and this workbook is intended to be that way for you.

This is a workbook, so the expectation is you will need to put in some work in order to see the fruit. So, who are you?

Self-Assessment to find your baseline

This framework will help you to apply your purpose and a sense of purpose. As you may recall from The Dream Book, your sense of purpose may not be all good. You may feel a sense of purpose for things that are ultimately not beneficial to you. As you take time to fill out the self-assessment to find your baseline, keep in mind that your feelings might not be a part of your divine purpose pertaining to your thoughts, self-perceptions, and motivations. So rather than taking this self-assessment as fast as you can, try to see it as more of a present-day perception of yourself. This neutral realization will help to keep you from drawing lines of absolutes, while still realizing the potential within the things where you find purpose and meaning. We find the most good in our sifting of thoughts about our sense of purpose and our divine purpose.

Natural and physical giftings

_____

_____

_____

Spiritual gifting

_____

_____

_____

Talents and abilities

_____

_____

_____

Developed skill sets

_____

_____

_____

Desires

_____

_____

_____

*What are your passions?*_____

_____

What are your callings? _____

_____

What do you love to do? _____

_____

*What are you born for?*_____

_____

*What is your education?*_____

_____

What are you internally driven to do?

_____

_____

_____

What bothers you most?

_____

_____

_____

What are your top 10 strengths?

_____

_____

_____

What are your top 10 fears?

_____

_____

_____

What is success to you right now?

_____

_____

_____

What is failure to you right now?

_____

_____

_____

What is your current emotional state? When did it start, and why?

_____

_____

_____

What are your top 10 values? Why?

_____

_____

_____

What are your top 10 goals? Why?

_____

_____

_____

Now we're going to take the following list of the true and divine purposes and self-assess what goes into that.

Divine/True Purpose:

1. *Our Divine Purpose comes from Godly values, promises, mandates, and prophecy, all geared to bring us life.*

2. *Our Divine Purpose brings noticeably good fruit to the people around us in small and big ways.*

3. *Our Divine Purpose is recognizable to the people around us as something that is part of our life/calling.*

4. *Our Divine Purpose grows because of how we do something, even more than what we do.*

5. *Our Divine Purpose is mirrored by the life and eternal purpose of Jesus.*

6. *Our Divine Purpose brings meaning and a compounding "good" to our life.*

7. *Our Divine Purpose is built on established truth, not feelings.*

8. *Our Divine Purpose is rarely short-term in application because God is eternal.*

9. *Our Divine Purpose is something you invest your time, talents, and gifts into, not something that comes out of nowhere.*

10. *Our Divine Purpose should create compounding feelings of satisfaction and enjoyment as we invest in it.*

Let's take some time to evaluate the preceding answers that compose your sense of purpose and compare them with the divine purpose list. Read through your list to see if anything disagrees with the divine purpose list. For example, do any of your desires, passions, or things that you feel like you were born for, etc., disagree with the divine purpose list? Now write down everything on the following lines that disagrees with the divine purpose list so that you can sort it out and give yourself a mindful exercise to things that are potentially in disagreement within yourself.

1._____

2._____

3._____

4._____

5._____

6._____

7._____

8._____

9._____

10._____

Write out your divine purpose as a third party bio that is at least one paragraph long.

_____

_____

_____

This is an important exercise to help you identify the things you might be working through. You may be unaware of something deep inside that potentially disagrees with your divine purpose. That's okay. We're all working to apply ourselves cognitively, actionably, and proactively to become better people. Also, we are just processing these thoughts as an exercise. We are not creating absolutes here. We are working through the shifting of our thoughts, feelings, desires, and our emotions so that we can be more mindful of our true sense of purpose. And as we perfect this ability to sift through our propensities and maybe our fears to get to the things that drive us to become a better person, we are strengthening our inner self and training our brains with the right elements within the dream.

If you realize today that fear is coming into your dreams in different ways, but it's not a part of your divine purpose, then fear should be approached differently than that of being self-identified. The fear is not who you are. It is something you are feeling. It is something that is communicating. Who you are is in your identity and within your true purpose.

You may have written down a few things that bother you. That's okay. Remember, we're not creating everlasting labels here. We are only being mindful of our present-day moment and how we think and feel. These thoughts and feelings might change tomorrow. However, for some of you, these thoughts and feelings may have been around for a really long time. And if that is the case, then it's something that you should be diving into to explore and resolve. Those everlasting messages will carry into your dream life in perpetuity. It's best if you confront them slowly, methodically, and thoroughly.

Suppose you have had a perpetuating fear of falling since you were a child. It may show up in every one of your dreams or in your important dreams. Do you see how your past framework and thoughts can affect your future dream life? It's essential to see how our past affects our future dreams. The goal here is to resolve any elements that take away from the neutrality of receiving future dreams. It's fantastic to receive dreams that relate to our past that help us to understand our present and future contexts. However, it would be a bummer if we kept reliving the same fears in the same situation because they're unresolved rather than unlocking our dream's future or present-day potential. That is why we take the time to separate and sort the inner workings of ourselves to find the healthy parts and to bring healing to the hurt parts.

Write out one in 400 trillion_____

That is the odds of you being born with your parents alone. That does not consider your grandparents and your great-grandparents and all those that preceded them. You should feel really special to be alive right now.

CHAPTER 1

SPAGHETTI ON THE WALL

This chapter is designed around the concept of throwing spaghetti on the wall. If you take spaghetti and throw it on the wall, you will get to see what sticks. In the past, this was a way people used to determine if the pasta was al dente. They would pull it right out of a hot pot and throw it on the wall. If it stuck, then it's done. With our dreams, we don't want to take that approach. We don't want to pursue Google for our dreams, definitions, context, and clarity. We don't even want to use dictionaries or dream dictionaries to help us understand. Our dreams are built around us. That's why we took so much time on the assessments to work out your baseline.

As you might have picked up in The Dream Book, there is a correlation of responsibility built around the individual, and the main focus is not to externalize your solutions but to internalize them. We need to look within to find the answers, not outside ourselves but inside ourselves. So as you dive into your heart, mind, emotions, and fears, and into your hopes and dreams, you will begin to find the answers that you are looking for. This is not for you to go into an introspective disaster journey looking for every bad thing. You will go on a guided journey to help you find solutions and meaning at the end. You have my permission to continue to throw spaghetti on the wall. Just don't do it to try to define your dreams.

Personal Agreement

Write out a list of five things you can't live without. These five things you can't live without could be a part of your list of personal agreements.

1._____

2._____

3._____

4._____

5._____

Add a list of five things that everybody should do.

1._____

2._____

3._____

4._____

5._____

It is helpful to know those things that we have a propensity to. Personal agreements can be anything from coffee to working hard, hanging out with friends on the weekends, and watching Hallmark movies. We all have different personal agreements, and it's essential to know which ones we have because they influence the way we dream. As a reminder, personal agreements do not validate something as true. Personal agreements are simply what you have agreed to align yourself with, believe, or like to do. Truth is another equation. Personal agreements speak to the propensities that we have. Some personal agreements we have are good for us, and others may not be

From this list of colors and styles, which one can you relate to most often?
Red, blue, green, orange, yellow, white, black, pink, purple, vibrant, muted, grayscale

_____

_____

What kinds of movies do you relate to the most? Action, drama, comedy, documentaries, indy...etc?

_____

_____

Sorting Mail

Write down the top 10 thoughts that you had yesterday on the list below? Don't fill in any dates yet.

1._____ date _____

2. _____ date _____

3._____ date _____

4._____ date _____

5._____ date _____

6._____ date _____

7._____ date _____

8._____ date _____

9._____ date _____

10._____ date _____

How many of them are the same thoughts that you are having today? How many of them are the same thoughts that you had last week? This exercise aims to help you identify when those thoughts started happening and also to realize that you may be carrying over thoughts from the previous day or week, which could be keeping you from having new thoughts today.

Return to the list of 10 thoughts you had yesterday and put a date by each of them roughly around the time you started having that thought. This exercise will help you to identify the origin of those thoughts. This is a really cool exercise we need to utilize in our dream lives because we have all these experiences and thoughts in our dreams, and if we don't know where they came from or when they started, then we'll be confused.

Spirit, Soul, and Body Dreams

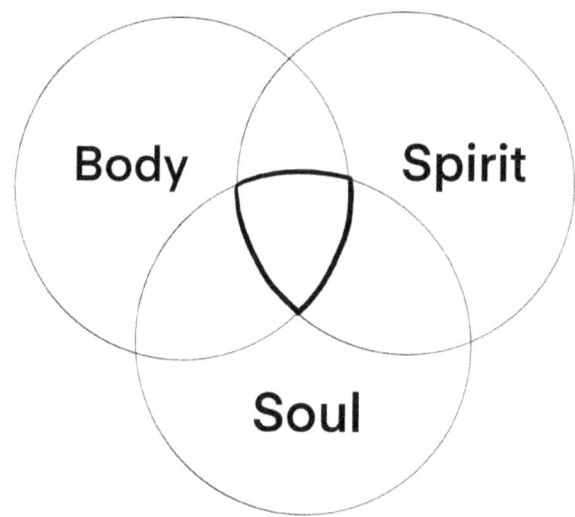

There are three different primary origins of dreams, which are from your spirit, your soul, and your body. As referenced from The Dream Book below, you can see how each area affects your dreams specifically. You can most definitely have a dream incorporating more than one area, like simultaneously having a dream from your body and soul. Although your spirit, soul and body are different aspects of who you are, when it comes to your dreams, they can overlap in tremendous ways. Nevertheless, we all need to identify where our dreams come from. Once we know where the dream starts, we can know where it's going. Read over the list below, and let's practice identifying the origin of dreams.

Body dreams: these are dreams that come from your body. If you're sick, you can dream about how you feel physically. Our physical body can really affect our dreams. If you have the flu, this can really impact the type of dreams you'll have, as well as if you take medication for the sickness. Let's say you have a broken arm; because of the pain in your arm, you could have a dream about your arm. These types of dreams are just processing what the body is going through. It's also interesting to note that if you're pregnant, this can impact your dreams because once it's developed enough, the baby is dreaming, and while you are dreaming, things can get mixed up.

Soul dreams: these are dreams that come from your wants and desires. These dreams will be filled with the things you want from life, e.g., a car, house, or money. In these types of dreams, you would get the car you want, the house you want, etc. You may have a dream and be asked to play guitar in a band because you're the best guitarist in the world. These types of dreams are easy to notice, and they're connected to your wants and desires. These are not the types of dreams that we're going to be talking about in this book.

Spirit dreams: these are dreams that come from God. It's easy to notice these dreams because they usually call us to something greater than we are or ever thought we could be. Joseph, from the Bible, dreamed he was going to be the leader of his family, and he was the youngest son. This seems like a soul dream because how could that be? It doesn't make any sense. But this is what he was called to do and who he was called to be. It was more significant than anything he could have imagined. Healthy God's dreams will always call you up to a higher place in your life and into your calling. Part of spiritual dreams is that they bring correction to how we perceive ourselves and others. God has a plan for our life. These dreams will guide us to that plan and even show us the plan.

Here are five different dreams. Each dream comes from a different place. Identify where these dreams come from.

1. Someone under a water fall guzzling water.

2. Driving without touching the wheel and your vehicle changes.

3. Giant tree branching out and producing good and bad fruit

_____

4. Teeth falling out

_____

5. Skydiving

_____

Spiritual dream example:

Snakes = lies, accusations, manipulation, enticement...

If you only see the snake, you're being influenced or manipulated into believing a lie.

If you are bitten by the snake, you have been impacted or you're believing a lie about yourself or others. Stop believing negative things. This is a warning dream to be aware of what and who you are listening to.

Soul dream example:

We get the dream wrong when we think we're having a dream about the person, for example it's your boss, and it's very negative. If you are having problems at work the dream is a soul dream in which you are processing the way you're feeling about your boss. Your boss has nothing to do with the dream, but everything to do with you. The dream is reflecting your anger, disappointment, or rejection... You need to bless your boss and move on.

Body dream example:

If you sprained your ankle, it's not uncommon to have a dream about your foot at some point during the healing process. This is because your foot may be throbbing and is causing pain during the night, as well as the trauma you have gone through.

Now its your turn. Write out three different kinds of dreams.

Write out an example of a spiritual dream that you may have had.

_____

_____

_____

_____

_____

_____

_____

Write out an example of a soul dream that you may have had.

_____

_____

_____

_____

_____

_____

_____

_____

Write out an example of a body dream that you may have had.

_____

_____

_____

_____

_____

_____

_____

This is great practice. Keep this in mind as you continue to dream. You will be surprised when your body talks to you about something verses when your spirit talks to you about something. The more we know where things come from, the better we can understand where they are going.

Inventory Your Cords of Agreement

Thoughts + Desires = Cord of Agreement

What agreements do you have that define your life today? Let's look at the primary things you feel most aligned with. We absolutely couldn't detach from the way we define agreements based on what we believe and think today. Perhaps you think about something often throughout the day or week. It's something you may actually obsess over in a good way. It's an agreement that you have cyclical or firm thoughts about. I want you to think about agreements that shape your behavior in both monumental and in simple ways. For example, unbreakable covenants that you have and your favorite ice cream.

Here are some common cords of agreement that are tied to our dream life:

- Any forms of agreements
    - What you like, what you love, what you surround yourself with, etc.
- Agreements with fears
    - Fear of failure, not being good enough, confidence, fear of lack, etc.
- The unconscious, preconscious, and conscious state
    - Thoughts that your mind is producing
- Agreements about who you are or who you are not
    - Preconceived ideas about who you are and who you have identified to be
- Any forms of covenants
    - Commitments and covenants that you have agreed to. Whom you are married to, friends with, etc.
- Soul ties
    - Past and present relationships, especially those involving intimacy
- Agreements in proximity
    - You live in a certain city, neighborhood, region, or country

Write out a list of your top 10 good cords of agreement. Don't worry, you can change them later. They don't all have to be profound. Perhaps some of you feel very strongly about never being late. That could be one of your cords of agreement. Or, some of you spend a whole lot of time thinking about chocolate, more time than others do. That could be one of your cords of agreement.

1._____

2._____

3._____

4._____

5._____

6._____

7._____

8._____

9._____

10._____

Write out 10 not-so-good cords of agreement that you have. These are things you know you have the propensity to do or agree with that you don't like. These may be your thoughts, and they also could be thoughts that are not yours that you tend to dwell on. Now cords of agreements come from different places, so we are not assigning blame to anyone. Even if you have a cord of agreement that is not so good, pinpointing it right now will actually help you down the road. For instance, while reading this you recall one of your fears. You know that fear is not the best to have, but it is a fear that you have, and it's something you have had for a long time. Perhaps that fear helped you out at different times., But, ultimately it's not the best to have because you would prefer to live in freedom. Well, write down that fear because it is something that you may have a cord of agreement in. This exercise is between you and this book. You can be as truthful as you would like to be with yourself. The more truthful you are, the better off you will be to interpret and resolve your dreams.

1._____

2._____

3._____

4._____

5._____

6._____

7._____

8._____

9._____

10._____

Now, take these 20 cords of agreement and draw a sleeping person lying on the ground. That is you sleeping. Draw out these 20 agreements over your sleeping self. Have them hover over you. Some will draw an ice cream cone over your head, and others will draw relationships that are unbreakable or very strong ideals that you may have. This exercise is done so that you can visually see the cords of the agreement you have in your life. We are now mindfully aware that these cords of agreement produce elements that may affect our dream life in monumental ways. These are things that we have agreed to hear about and think about. We have agreed to hear from them whether they are good or bad.

Now let's visualize these 20 agreements affecting you as you sleep. Take one of the agreements and double it in size. Now that agreement is affecting you twice as much as it was before? How much would your sleep change? Would you receive more or less of that agreement? More, of course. Now take one of the bad agreements and remove it. How many times would you see that agreement in your dreams now? None, right? It's been removed. The goal of this exercise is for you to identify your cords of agreement and realize

that you have the power to maximize and magnify them, and you have the power to eliminate them. If you have cords of agreement that affect you negatively and take away from your life, it will significantly benefit you to resolve them. I know many people pursue life coaching, counseling, and self-help books to help with resolving past trauma. Others pursue spiritual fact books to help them with their fears. Regardless of how you see fit to address your negatively influential cords of agreement, it all starts with an idea. A thought that points us to the ideal situation, the ideal solution. As you take those negative thoughts captive, you are wielding your power over that idea. You can choose to magnify it, or you can choose to eliminate it by resolving it. We have more power than we think we do as it pertains to our thoughts and our desires.

Let's produce two hypothetical new cords of agreements.

Scenario one: A new relationship starts to form. The couple has lots of thoughts about connecting and living together. Desire is birthed. Now the dreams can start. Do you see this relationship cord?

Scenario Two: You have a falling out with an old best friend. You start thinking about how they should be punished for what they did to you. Desire is shaped, and dreams can start. The next time you have a dream about beating someone up, it is justified by the feelings you have. A new cord is established.

Now it is your turn. Write two scenarios using the same framework to establish a cord of agreement. Thoughts + Desires = Cord of Agreement. The whole point of this exercise is for you to be able to create and identify cords of agreement.

Scenario one:

Scenario two:

CHAPTER 2

THE STUDY

Building Your Own Dream House

Everyone speaks a unique language. It is common to you, but not so common to everyone else. This gives us a unique advantage to understanding ourselves versus having someone else trying to understand what we are saying. The same is true for our dream language. We have a unique language for how we receive dreams and how we perceive them. This language is developed in part by ourselves and can only be interpreted by using the framework that designed it.

There is no shortcut to understanding ourselves. We can be complex, at times. That is why we are going to take some time to build out a visual working model of the things we find fitting in our life. We are going to create a room for certain sections of our life. In today's exercise you are going to build your own dream house. This is a framework that you can use even beyond this workbook. It will help you to think abstractly about your thoughts, emotions, and life.

This was the tool that accelerated my ability to interpret dreams because I was able to visualize my dream house. The house was a full representation of who I am and each room was a different part of me. I could properly define each room and how it served me, and identify the purpose of each element inside that room.

Your dream house is a collaboration of your imagination, self-perceptions, hopes, and your present world. Don't overthink it. You are creating a visualization of the world that you currently live in. When I say world, I mean your perceptions, hopes, dreams, aspirations, and realities. Your dream house can change and adapt over time. Nothing is absolute in your dream house. However, because your dream house is built around your ideas, self-perceptions, hopes and dreams it has a tendency to carry over throughout time.

Let's go into each room and build correlations between the physical elements that are in that room and how you see the world through your own eyes.

Take this page and draw a blueprint of your house just as an architect would. Identify each room just as you would with your own house. Where is the kitchen? How many bathrooms are there? Where is the primary bedroom? As soon as you are done laying out the blueprint we will get into the specifics of each room.

When you start the layout of each room, ask yourself the following two questions. How do I see myself in that room? How big is each room? These questions need to be asked at the same time because the dream house is you. You are trying to create a visualization for you in the form of a house. The size of your living room is a reflection of you. Consider these two questions as you draw out each room in the blueprint of your dream house.

Let's look at the common rooms. If you have other rooms that are not in this common list, go ahead and write them down below.

Bedroom

Bathrooms

Hallway

Kitchen

Office

Outside areas

Living room

Laundry room

Other rooms

_____

_____

Now we are going to look at the characteristics within each room. But, we are only going to highlight a few of the characteristics that go into each room. It is really up to you to go through and self-define all of the little details. In The Dream Book I go into some very specific details for each room. I want you to be able to do that for yourself. Take your time and think deeply about those specifics because they will be profound to you as you approach your next dream. I have given you some questions below as a prompt for each of the main rooms. Don't take this as a complete exercise until you have asked yourself if you see anything else in that room. Throughout my life, I have added details to each room every year. I have also changed some of the rooms that I have had based on changing situations in my life.

This is not just a simple exercise about making a playful little house. You are exercising your ability to think symbolically and signify yourself in a living structure. This living structure is very much like your dream life. Hopefully you will be able to see the profound nature of visualizing your own dream house.

Bedroom

How many beds do you have in your room? Whose pictures are on the wall? What colors did you choose? How big is your room? How many windows are there?? What floor of your house is your bedroom on? How many other bedrooms do you have? Who else is living in those bedrooms? How many pillows do you have on your bed? Do you have lights on the ceiling or just lamps?

_____

_____

_____

_____

Bathrooms

How big is your bathroom? What is it made out of? Do you have a bathtub and or do you have a shower? How many sinks do you have in your bathroom? Do you have items that are layed out or do you put everything away?

_____

_____

_____

_____

Hallway

What kind of pictures are in your hallway? How big is your hallway? What temperature do you set your hallway at?

_____

_____

Kitchen

How big is the kitchen? Is it modern or old? What is distinctly different from the kitchen that you currently have and this one? What kinds of silverware and cookware are present?

_____

_____

_____

_____

Office

Continue describing the characteristics of this room. Why is it distinctly yours and what is different about it? What do you see when you look at the floor and or the ceiling? Does it feel cramped or inviting? Is there a laptop, or books? If so, how many?

_____

_____

_____

_____

Outside areas

Describe the characteristics of the outside areas. You may have many of these, so take your time and detail them out.

_____

_____

_____

_____

Living room

Describe the characteristics of this room. How many chairs does it have and what are their orientations? How big is it?

_____

_____

_____

_____

Laundry room

Describe the characteristics of this room. What does it look like?

_____

_____

_____

_____

Other rooms

_____

_____

_____

_____

Dream Messengers

Dream messengers are a vehicle for how we are to receive the dreams. If you are receiving your dream through symbols, images, riddles, etc., it will help you to interpret it if you know what the vehicle is. Not every dream is the same and the vehicles in which the messages are delivered vary based on the individual and the dream that they have.

In this exercise we are going to review the various messengers and come up with examples of each one that would give us elements of our dream. This section will become the backdrop for how you interpret your dreams. If you assign the wrong messenger to your dream, the dream's interpretation will be lost in the confusion. Almost everyone makes this mistake early on in dream interpretation. For example, they have a dream and the messenger is signified, but instead of interpreting the dream using signified they interpret the dream using literal. In this case, the dream interpretation would be lost in the confusion. That is by far the most common misinterpretation that exists today.

Review each definition and create three examples within each one.

Signified

To be a sign, to point to, to represent something else.

1._____

2._____

3._____

Symbol

A representation of something else. An icon or window of understanding that points to something greater. For example, the icons on a desktop computer open up greater possibilities once the icon is clicked on.

1._____

2._____

3._____

4._____

Jargon

A word or phrase that is not formal or literary and typically used in ordinary or familiar conversation. The use of ordinary or familiar words or phrases. "The colloquialisms of the streets." For example, I wasn't born yesterday. Put your money where your mouth is.

1._____

2._____

3._____

Dialect

A dialect is a language spoken in the area you are from or a widely used saying that is figurative in meaning and different from the saying's literal meaning. An example is, "To bite off more than you can chew." This would mean that you tried to do something which is too difficult for you.

1._____

2._____

3._____

Metaphor

A figure of speech in which a word or phrase is applied to an object or action to which it is not literally applicable. You see a car in a dream. A car in a dream represents your gifts, talents, and abilities. The dream might not be about the car, but about your gifts, talents, and abilities. Your gifts, talents, and abilities also get you to where you want to be, just as a car does.

1._____

2._____

3._____

Veiled Language

Some of our dreams seem to be telling us something that we are not able to see or understand. Veiled language is not openly shown or stated. It is not expressed in a way that is clear and direct. It's hidden and you have to learn how to see it.

1._____

2._____

3._____

Non-Sequitur

A conclusion or a statement that does not logically follow the previous argument or statement. Dreams sometimes seem to have these vignettes that go from one to another, and they don't seem to make any sense. However, a closer look often reveals that it is the same dream at a different location and from a different point of view. While you are learning your dream language, be on the lookout for these types of dreams. Other times, it could be a different dream altogether. So, remember the learning curve you are on and be patient with yourself. This language can be difficult at first.

1._____

2._____

3._____

Paradox

A seemingly absurd or self-contradictory statement or proposition that, when investigated or explained, may prove to be well founded or true. For example, a person that stops going to work but makes more money from their business. You may have a dream like this and find it hard to believe. It does seem unreasonable or illogical, but sometimes the workers can get more done when the boss isn't in the room looking over their shoulder micromanaging everything that is being done.

1._____

2._____

3._____

4._____

Caricature

A picture, description, or imitation of a person in which certain striking characteristics are exaggerated in order to create a comic or grotesque effect. When you have these types of dreams, look at what is being exaggerated, and you will find out the meaning of the dream. When you have a dream and you have a very big nose, this dream could tell you that you have great discernment. With your nose, you can tell if the food is good or bad.

1._____

2._____

3._____

4._____

Implied Language

It is suggested, but not directly expressed; implicit. This is a big part of dream language. Look for clues that are hidden between the lines or concealed. Suggested, but not directly expressed. Look at what is understated, exaggerated, or blown out of proportion for better or worse than in reality.

1._____

2._____

3._____

Dark Speech

A statement or image has to be searched out in order to be discovered. This is a big part of dream language! Dreams that give you a deep desire to know the interpretation often have a lot more to say to you during the journey of understanding the meaning of the dream than the dream itself. This is a big part of dream life.

1._____

2._____

3._____

Allegory

A story or picture that you can interpret and find a hidden meaning. The story of Jonah and the whale, in the Bible, represents Jesus' death and resurrection. Jonah was three days and three nights in the belly of the whale, so the Son of Man was three days and three nights in the heart of the earth.

1._____

2._____

3._____

Literal

Not exaggerating or being metaphorical, but plainly stated, and able to be perceived easily.

These types of dreams are actually most often visions. The night visions will usually be fulfilled in the next few days. The vignette will play out just as you saw it in the night vision. It will literally happen. You may be the type who has literal night visions 80% of the time, and the other 20%, has dreams. This is a rare gift.

1._____

2._____

3._____

Here are five dreams. Please identify the vehicle that each dream is being delivered in.

Veiled Language – vehicle: _____

Dreams are hidden in story form. Think of the story as the package your gift comes in. Don't get lost inside the "package" or story that the dream is in. You are looking for the gift inside…the direction, the answer or solution. It's there for you, hidden in plain sight. When you have a dream where you need to purchase something but you think it costs too much so you don't buy it and just walk away. The interpretation is you are not ready to invest in yourself so you can enter into the next season.

Metaphor Dream – vehicle: _____

I'm driving in a car with my friend Marc in the passenger seat. Ginny was in the back. All of a sudden huge waves appeared in front of us. The waves kept coming and getting bigger. I rolled down my window and began to yell at the people to get ready for what was going to happen. Some of the people I saw in detail. I was thinking I'm yelling so loud Marc might get mad, but he was okay with it. Dream interpretation: My car represents my gifts, talents and abilities. I see future events in dreams. The waves would represent problems or events that were going to affect everyone around me, my city and country. I'm trying to tell everyone around me that there's going to be very difficult times ahead. Some of them I would know and lots of others I wouldn't. My friend Marc is a mentor to me. He was okay with the methods that I was using.

Allegory Dream – vehicle: _____

I was waiting in the dark and couldn't see how to get out of where I was. A man came and asked me why I haven't moved yet. I replied, "because I can't see where I'm going." I knew there were lots of things in my way and I needed some light, so I could see how to get out.

Literal Dream – vehicle: _____

Not exaggerating or being metaphorical, but plainly stated, and able to be perceived easily.

Sometimes a dream is very simple. You hear a voice telling you to call your friend. When you wake up and call them, you find out that they are having a problem and need your help.

Implied Language – vehicle: _____

Let's say you have a dream that you're being chased by giants. The giants are running so fast after you that it seems like they will catch you any second. You keep looking back with fear to see how close they are to you and you notice that they are wearing clothes with dollar signs on them. The interpretation of this dream is that you're having financial problems and you feel like you are in over your head. You're feeling the pressure of the debt and it's overwhelming.

These vehicles are pivotal to understanding the message inside the dream because it tells you how to interpret the dream. If the vehicle is literal then your interpretation will be led by the vehicle. If the vehicle is symbolic then it will assist you in interpreting your dream in a symbolic nature. After you have had some practice identifying the vehicles that your dreams are being delivered in, you should take a few steps back and find out where they came from. That would be your dream origin. In the dream book we talked about this in greater detail, but I will reference the main points here in this exercise.

Where did your dream come from?

Let us review a few dream origins so you can identify where the messengers are coming from.

- Divine purpose

  - Can come from any origin or any angle. All dreams stem from the protraction of your divine purpose. They work for or against your purpose. Your divine purpose is vast. It can be something small or very expansive as it connects to your life.

Some common cords of agreement you will see in divine purpose are:

- Proximity: You are living in a certain city, your neighborhood, region, or country.

  - People: Learning about your past, present, and future connection to people.

  - Self-defining: Truth establishing dreams, mindsets, learning about yourself, your gifts, skills, and thoughts.

  - Situations: Unlocking the nuggets of truth and lessons from the past or providing a glimpse into the future

- Demonic

  - The juxtaposition of having a divine purpose. You can be lost, tormented, oppressed or mistreated. You get the idea. The origin of these dreams can be very dark and taxing to wake up from. They are often immersive, intrusive, and alarming and ultimately can lead you away from your divine purpose. Not all dark dreams are demonic. Remember, it's not the messenger; it's the origin.

- Emotions

  - All 66 emotions (see Jeremy and Dr. Ally Butrous at drallybutrous.com on that resource) can be the originator of your dreams.

  - Sadness, fear (any fear), pleasure, joy, contentment, anger, etc. A huge source of many of our dreams is pointing out our emotional state.

  - Your thoughts from your unconscious, preconscious, and conscious states of mind

  - Thinking about not finishing laundry before bed can produce dreams about overwhelming laundry. Also, thinking about a problem at work can produce dreams that help solve the problem.

- Spirit

  - Our spirit is the source of many of the dreams that tie us into our ultimate purpose in life. It helps us avoid huge mistakes and speaks to us in monumental ways.

- Soul
  - Our soul is the source of updates from ourselves, our connections, relationships, and past relationships, especially those involving intimacy.

- Body
  - Your body is the source of dreams directly connected to your body. Is there a problem somewhere? Are you getting a hormone surge and your body is trying to tell you something? Did you have physical trauma, and your body is not done processing this? Is your body telling you that you have a sex drive? Is your body trying to let you know about a health issue?

- Garbage Pizza
  - There's no rhyme, no reason, no connection to your purpose, and no application to derive from the dream. It's a mess, and it can be trashed when a dream is identified as a "garbage pizza" dream. The best thing to do is throw it away and forget about it.

Here are five dreams. Please identify each dream's origin.

Divine Purpose Dream.

I was standing in front of a glass case. Inside the case were glass shelves and on the shelves were different style wallets. I looked at them for a while and chose the one I really wanted. I was asking the man behind the counter to show me the one I wanted. He said, "I've chosen this one for you." I was grieved. I didn't like it at all. I looked up to see who was talking to me and I knew it was God... I knew that this would be my calling for life.

_____

_____

_____

Demonic Dream.

The experiences we have in nightmares, fear, a sense of foreboding for the future and torment. Nightmares will not have color. Often people who have nightmares frequently will stop dreaming. The reason why they're afraid to dream is because they might have a nightmare. They often have to do with the fear of death. Any dream that you have that has no redeeming value and makes you afraid to dream again is demonic. A dream with a big spider in your room would be a demonic type of dream. The spider would represent a negative spirit trying to influence you.

_____

_____

_____

_____

Emotional Dream.

You are having a dream and you're falling and can't stop. This would give you a sense of your life being out of control. The metaphor is that you don't feel like you have anywhere or anyone to turn to. You are all alone and keep falling, and have nothing to hold on to. This type of dream could be after a breakup with someone or losing a job. Your emotions are dealing with the loss and it's being processed as you sleep.

_____

_____

_____

_____

Spirit Dream

In this dream, I was boarding a flight. The plane was very futuristic and had all kinds of luxuries and high technology. I got to my seat and prepared for take off. There was an elderly man seated next to me. When the plane took off, I was looking out of the window and noticed we were flying very low. I was frightened because we were flying just above the trees. I looked over at the man next to me and asked him if it is okay to fly this low? He smiled and said to me, "This is the safest way to fly!" I knew the interpretation as soon as he answered me. The metaphor of flying in a dream is that you have the ability to move in the spirit. To fly low would be to stay under the radar and notdraw attention to yourself. This way you will be able to do many things without being noticed and it keeps you humble.

_____

_____

_____

Dream Sequence

Practice a dream sequence that starts with a new origin each time. Once the origin is selected, insert one or two vehicles, and insert the dream.

Step One: Select an origin

Step Two: Select a vehicle

Step three: Insert the dream

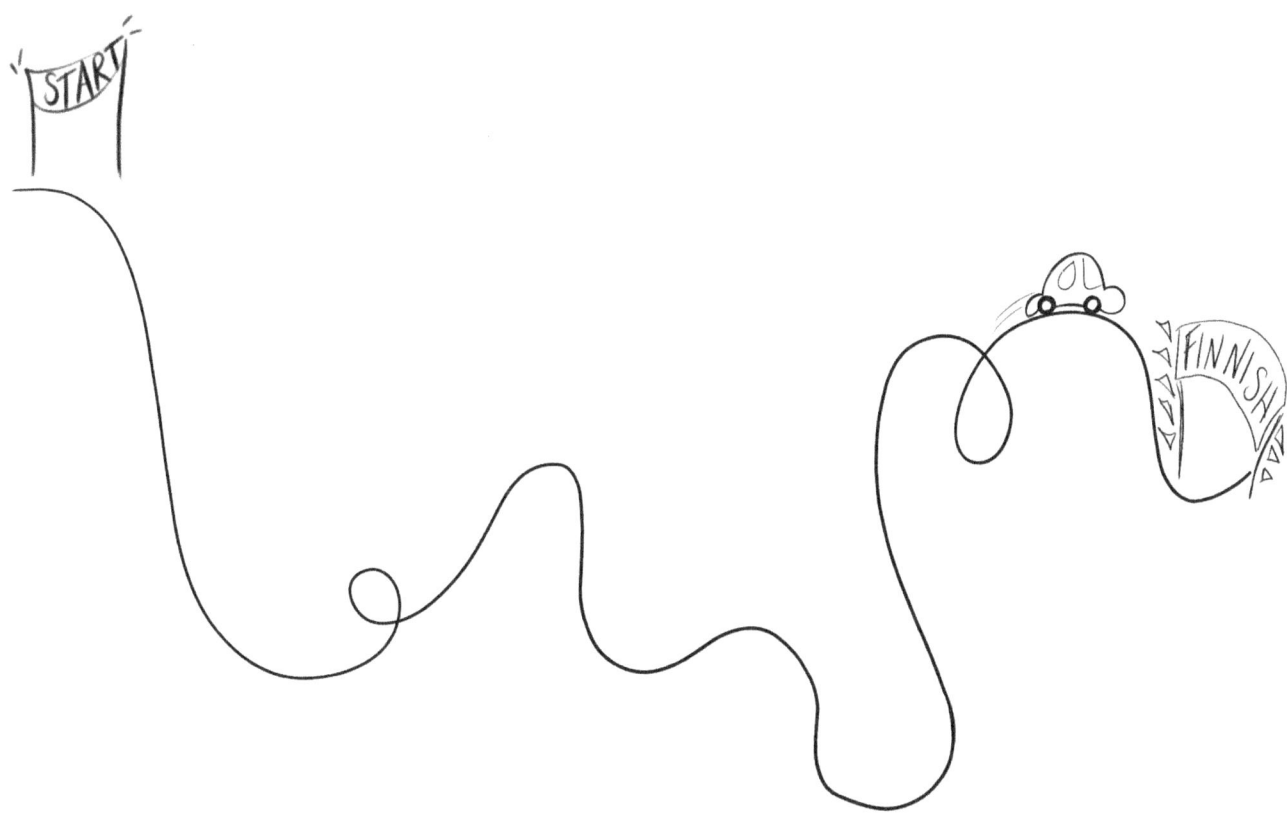

List of Origins:

Divine Purpose   Soul

Demonic   Body

Emotions   Garbage Pizza

Spirit

List of Vehicles:

Signified   Veiled Language   Implied Language

Symbol   Non Sequitur   Dark Speech

Jargon   Paradox   Allegory

Dialect   Caricature   Literal

Metaphor

Practice by doing 5 mix and match.

Step One: Select an origin

Step Two: Select a vehicle

Step three: Insert the dream

1._____

2._____

3._____

4._____

5._____

One of the most common mistakes here is that people will take real examples from their dream and not apply the proper signified, symbolic approach because they see the real examples. Signified and symbolic are the means of interpretation, but it doesn't mean that the element is not real. For example, you could have a dream about your father. He is a real person. You know him well. However, in your dream he represents something. He is displaying to you an element, an idea, a perspective. He is not showing up to you to parent you as your real father in your dream. So, just because you see something that's real doesn't mean that it's not significant or symbolic.

Most people come from the framework that if they see something real in their dream then it must be interpreted literally. That's not how the dream world works. Your dreams are only a composite of the things that you know or can imagine. Your dreams come from the same framework that creates your present-day reality. If you see something that's real it doesn't mean that it's literal.

CHAPTER 3

PERCEPTION

Building out your dream language is establishing relatable, valuable meanings and perceptions of a person, place, or thing. This points to that. This thing means that. This thing opens up this door of thought.

As I approach my dreams and their contents, my heart and mind need to carry a basic care and value for what my dreams are saying. I like to tell myself, "Okay dream, I am open to hearing you out." That is a fundamental value that I am giving a place in my heart and mind to have more dreams and go deeper into their understanding. The exact value you should have for your dreams as a whole should trickle down into the elements of the dream.

We perceive not with our eyes, but with our mind. Your interpretation of what you see in a dream is based on your perception of those elements in your mind.

Symbolic, Signified, and Literal

Let's evaluate a few keywords as we start to perceive dreams differently. A symbol is an isolated symbol. Symbolic is a process of serving as a symbol. Signified is the meaning or idea expressed by a sign, pointing to a sign, or a symbol. Literal is the process of evaluating things in their most basic sense without metaphor; it's strict and factual

Let's evaluate some bread using the three available perceptions. First we have bread that is symbolic. Secondly, we have bread that is signified. Lastly, we have bread that is literal.

Symbolic Bread: The symbolic extension of the bread's meaning can be endless. I will provide you with one example for symbolic bread and I would like for you to do the same. Bread is symbolic for a growing child.

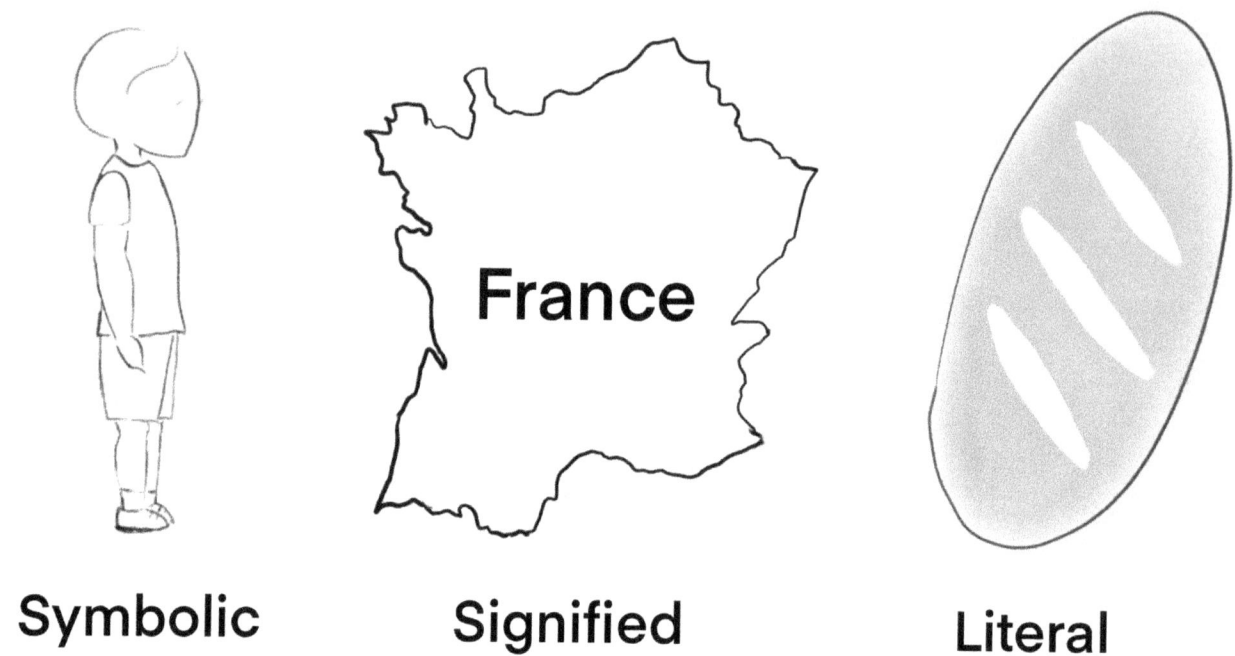

Do you see how bread is not the primary key in this interpretation, but rather the growing child? If the bread was gone then you would not have the growing child, so it is an essential part of the interpretation. However, bread is simply the means to achieving the understanding of a growing child.

What is your symbolic answer for bread?

_____

_____

_____

Signified Bread: Signified points to something whether it's symbolic or literal. It is a signpost. I will provide you with one example for signified bread and I would like for you to do the same. Bread signifies the country of France. In this example, bread is a signpost for a completely different reality much like in the symbolic understanding, signified can be an icon that opens up a door to a different reality. Signified can also point to very real things. This confuses most people because those very real realities are actually real. They automatically assume that because the interpretation signifies a real reality, then it must be interpreted literally. If our bread signifies the country of France, it validates the reality of France. The question for the interpreter would be, "What does France mean to you in this interpretation?"

What is your signified answer for bread?

_____

_____

_____

Literal Bread: Literal means the most basic interpretation without any metaphor, it's strictly factual. I will provide you with one example of literal bread and I would like for you to do the same. Literal bread is ciabatta bread. Literal is simple in its interpretive means. This ciabatta bread means ciabatta bread. Nothing symbolic or signified is to be added to its interpretation.

What is your answer for literal bread?

_____

_____

_____

_____

Dreams are 98% symbolic or signified and 2% literal meaning.

Let's practice some more. Below you will find a few categories. Write out an example of symbolic, signified, and literal interpretations.

Father

Symbolic _____

_____

Signified _____

_____

Literal _____

_____

Rainbow

Symbolic _____

_____

Signified _____

_____

Literal _____

_____

Gun

Symbolic _____

_____

Signified _____

_____

Literal _____

_____

What does your coffee cup mean?

This is a very simple exercise, but it will require you to develop your abstract thinking. We are going to go through this together, and then you are going to apply the concepts to your own symbolic journey. Remember, signified and symbolic doesn't mean that it's not literal. It simply means that it's pointing to something else, which can be figurative or imaginary, or an idea, or something that is literal.

Okay, go get a coffee cup and place it in front of you. Now, this coffee cup can represent many things. On one hand, it can be its intended self and be a coffee cup. You could fill it up with water and now it's a water cup. If you were outside and it was windy, you could use it as a paperweight. If you were to pick it up and throw it at someone, it could be a weapon. Do you see how this coffee cup can represent many things? It is not just a coffee cup. So if you were to look up what a coffee cup means in my dream, you would really be setting yourself up to get lost by using my definition tor interpret your dreams. You must understand what the coffee cup represents to you within the context of your dreams.

The framework for what the coffee cup represents comes from you. You have a special relationship with this coffee cup. Whether or not it's very detailed and formed yet, in the context of this dream, this coffee cup is important. Iit might speak to something subtle to help guide you 1% in the right direction or it may be the entire emphasis of your dream. In this exercise, I would like for you to look inside your heart and mind and come up with five different ways that this coffee cup could be represented. Please try and use new examples and not repeat the ones that I have already mentioned.

I want you to ask yourself what your coffee cup would mean. Place yourself in different situations in your mind, and take your coffee cup with you.

Please list out five examples of what your coffee cup could mean.

1._____

2._____

3._____

4._____

5._____

Okay, now that you have five examples of what your coffee cup could mean I want you to share why you specifically came up with those examples. Mind you, this is a personal exercise and you don't have to share this with anyone else. But in expressing your why, you will be self-defining a thought, an idea, or an emotion that you had, which can be tied to you personally and can also make you feel vulnerable. Some of these ideas could also be imaginary and part of your creative process.

Why did you choose these examples? List them out one through five. Perhaps you recalled a situation in the past, or an emotion that you felt, or an idea that you have related to something else.

1._____

2. _____

3._____

4._____

5._____

Did you list any examples of ones that came from your mind, emotions, or past experiences? If you did, fantastic! You came up with your own definitions of what your coffee cup could mean. This is a huge step in interpreting your dreams. Now, which examples were expressed to you the strongest? Which one stood out to you the most? Is it possible that those have a deep relatable experience that's tied to you? If so, go ahead and circle that example.

Are you able to differentiate the ones that stood out the most versus the ones that you are not really attached to? You are exercising your ability to think in abstraction and self-discovery. You are sorting out context and categories on this very simple exercise of what your coffee cup means. You are learning to differentiate the relatable experiences that could tie into your framework around what your coffee cup means. This is fantastic because this can be applied to every single thing that you see and experience in your dreams. Hopefully, you are able to glean not only into the stronger examples, but more so the relatable ones. I want you to be able to see the thing that you can relate to the most, and not just the thing that could be the most emotionally charging.

This is a practical exercise in expanding our local framework to come up with something that's abstract pertaining to a relatable object. As you begin to exercise your mind and the inquisitive nature of self-discovery you will begin to find the representations that you are inclined to believe. This also is the same framework that you build your perceptions and symbolic journeys on. When you see someone in your dream more often than not they are representative of something else. They are signified and speak to you of an idea, an emotion, a different person, a time, and a place. It's up to you to sort through these ideas based on the context of your dream. However, you will have many opportunities to practice because you will find commonalities within the dream language that you develop. are intended to know what your dreams mean. This is a very exciting opportunity to explore. As you settle this framework in your mind it will be much easier to interpret your dreams moving forward.

Breaking down a dream

Identify a personal interpretation of these 20 elements. Write down one word that each element represents or means to you. What do the elements signify to you? What do they represent?

20 different icons we could place on this page.

- Road _____
- Bread _____
- Bird _____
- Chair _____
- Wind _____
- Bed _____
- Pen _____
- Rainbow _____
- Bag _____
- Cake _____
- Car _____
- Book _____
- Hat _____
- Boat _____
- House _____
- Shirt _____
- Drink _____
- Computer _____
- Phone _____
- Glasses _____

Flip your perception exercise

You have identified the personal perception of the 20 identifiable icons. In this exercise, you will flip your perception to be the opposite of these 20 identifiable icons. List out your responses below to be the exact opposite of how you first perceived each one. The reason for this exercise is to expand your ability to perceive differently than the way that you have normally sought perception. For starters, your perception could be different from reality so you need to be able to change your perception accordingly. Secondly, the mental exercise to envision someone else's perception is inherently strengthening yours not to reaffirm or believe, but to teach us the fluidity in interpretation. List out your flipped perception responses below.

- Road _____
- Bread _____
- Bird _____
- Chair _____
- Wind _____
- Bed _____
- Pen _____
- Rainbow _____
- Bag _____
- Cake _____
- Car _____
- Book _____
- Hat _____
- Boat _____
- House _____
- Shirt _____
- Drink _____
- Computer _____
- Phone _____
- Glasses _____

What do you value?_____

_____

_____

_____

What we perceive in life spills over into our dreams. What do you value deeply? Animals? Vacation? Specialty coffee? Do you have a particular hobby that you love? Shopping? Gardening? Fishing? What do you spend your time doing the most? Watching TV? Which Shows? Working? Teaching your children? Who do you take advice from? What podcasts do you listen to? Whose books do you read? Write out the top ten things you value most.

1._____

2. _____

3._____

4._____

5._____

6._____

7._____

8._____

9._____

10._____

Within those 10 values, which ones do you see in your dreams? Place a checkmark next to the value you see in your dreams.

What angle are you viewing your dreams?

_____

_____

_____

Every season of life provides us with a different perspective. Perhaps, your symbolic imagery stays the same, but your perspective changes or your elevation changes. If you see something in your dream in the first person then the perspective is from your mind through your eyes. If you experience your dream through the eyes of a bird flying overhead then your perspective is looking down. Why is this important? It tells you everything you need to know about personal involvement, assignment and perspective.

Now, zoom out and draw out an aerial view of you holding a phone.

What did you learn about this exercise? Did you find in your first person sketch that you provided more detail in the small form? Did you find that in your aerial view you provided a wider frame of context? Did your aerial view include other people or other objects that your first person perspective didn't include? Every dream has a built-in perspective and it's very important that we identify the perspective provided and understand its intended meaning.

Representatives

Another way to understand signified and symbolic within your dreams is to apply a perspective of representation. It is another way to say meaning within meaning. If your father shows up in your dream he may, in fact, be your real father in life. The wrong automatic assumption is that your literal father is going to be factually walking out what you perceive. Rather, he is a representative in your dream to an idea, fact, emotion, belief, or behavior, etc. Perhaps, based on your relationship you perceive an emotion or an idea from the very presence of your father being in your dream.

Here are examples of a father being a representative in your dream. Fill in the blanks.

1. He represents authority

2. He represents generosity

3. He represents pain and suffering

4. He represents brokenness

5. He represents love

This is not an exhaustive list. Your father can represent anything, but it's specific to you. Your father and the perspective you have of your father in your dreams is inherently yours. I cannot stress enough that your father in your dream 98% of the time is symbolic or signified. It would be wrong to assume that your father is literally going to factually walk out what you perceive. He is a representative to something that you are processing.

With the understanding of representatives applied, list out five more examples of what your mother could represent in your dream. Fill in the blanks.

1. She represents compassion

2. She represents love

3. She represents our past

4. She represents anger

5. She represents life

6._____

7._____

8._____

9._____

10._____

CHAPTER 4

UNDERSTANDING YOUR DREAMS

We start your dream journey today. What are you made of today? It is a composite of you, the good, the bad, and the fantastic. It's all you. Your emotions, mindsets, mood, and past experiences are all fully alive in your dreams today. If you were to go to bed right now and start dreaming, your most present self would show up and contribute to your dreams. This is the starting line for your dreaming today, and it will be the same for tomorrow. This is good for us to know and for us to understand.

It is important to know that you have a role in your dream life and that you should take inventory of your situations, emotions, mindsets, and influences because they contribute to the way you see your dreams. This inventory can be as basic as being mindful of your current season, situations, or relationships, and how they are affecting you. Also, you can go so far as to inventory things that are off or seem to bother you, and that will paint a picture, as well, if you see them in your dreams. Who you are today is, and can be, a direct contributor to where you are going. This is the same as your destination or where you are going. Your destination is, by design, a composite of your gifts, talents, skill sets, abilities, desires, passions, callings, what you love to do, are born to do, what you were educated in, and what drives you during the day.

Most dreams talk to us in our current season of life (past 90-120 days) but are tied to the entirety of our life. When we are on the road in our dream journey, we will get different kinds of dreams to keep us on the road. We will receive instruction dreams, warning dreams, step-by-step dreams, flashbacks, or deja vu dreams.

Define your season

List out your current season focal points. What are your primary markers of importance for the past 90-120 days? What is pressing on your heart, mind, and emotions? What is new in the past 120 days? How is it different from the past season? You won't know how to interpret your dreams until you can self-define what season you are in.

Here is an example. John is stressed about his job right now. He is excited about relocating for work, but money is tight. He is ready for a bigger house because his family is growing. The house is very busy and his time is limited. He desires for his family to love him and he wants them to know that everyday.

Do you have a picture of the season of life that John is in? If he were to tell you about one of his dreams you could see this lens that he currently sees the world through.

List out the top 10 primary markers that define your current season. These can be emotions, situations, a representative, a problem, and or a dream.

1._____

2. _____

3._____

4._____

5._____

6._____

7._____

8._____

9._____

10._____

Look at your dreams in color.

Every color means something to us. Oftentimes a color can trigger or relate to an emotion. In a continuation of the primary markers that define your season from the preceding exercise, list out each marker and assign a color or colors to it. List out the ten markers that define your current season and color over them or write out what color is assigned to each. It is strongly recommended for you to actually color them so you can visualize each color on the paper.

1._____

2. _____

3._____

4._____

5._____

6._____

7._____

8._____

9._____

10._____

Do you notice a color pallet from your dreams? Each season will come with different colors.

Here is an example.

We're looking for the color of the signs…

We will use what we know to speak to us….

Yellow.... Caution, gift, fear, yield

Emotion connected fear or worry. Warning signs typically use a yellow background with black letters; most are diamond-shaped. Yellow warning signs alert you to hazards or changes in conditions ahead. Solution so we need to wait to make sure. We need to use our gift to make sure everything is in order and proceed with caution and alertness.

Red.... Stop, anger, love, passion

Emotion connected sadness anger. Red traffic signs convey traffic regulations that require drivers to take immediate action to avoid threats to traffic safety. A "Wrong Way" sign is an example of a traffic sign with a red background. Solution immediately stop and ask yourself why you're doing this. Spend some time praying and evaluating the situation and move forward when you know everything is safe and in order. Ginny and I were at a red light that was broken and had to go a different way to get free.

Green.... Go, growth, life

Emotion connected happiness joy. Signs with green backgrounds help direct motorists to places along the road or to destinations of general interest. Green background signs are informational. Solution continue as planned; be watching for other signs; and enjoy yourself. Stay focused on your goal, stay intentional.

Blue.... Revelation, insight, connected

Emotion connected peace contentment. Blue road signs are very commonly used to indicate that road user services are available nearby, such as tourist information. Solution use your gift and doors will open for you and all your needs will be taken care of. You are asking for insight and who you're supposed to connect with.

Orange....Passion, fire, warning, under construction

Emotion connected frustration. This color is used to alert you to possible dangers ahead due to construction and maintenance projects. Solution go forward with your passion, but understand that you are headed towards something that needs to be built and you are one of the builders so don't get frustrated. Remember it is going to take some time, but it will be worth it. You are also bringing the revelation to the table. Orange is unique and highly creative! Fire and passion are what we use to create all types of art! I think the visual arts come to us through our eyes!! So a vision would be apropos.

Types of Dreams

Direction Dreams:

Below is an example of a directional dream. List out the elements below that you can identify that are directional and what are the lessons provided.

Vivid or bright color = These dream colors are very bright and seem like real life as if you were really there!

Direction dreams should be interpreted with your "divine purpose as your lens" and in context with your other direction dreams. All these dreams in context should make sense with the trajectory of your life's calling. This will help you understand the metaphors being mixed with the literal applications... A lot of times warnings are mixed inside of direction dreams.

I dreamed about the high school my son would go to if we didn't move. The dream was very dark and seemed to be a warning that this high school wasn't a good fit for my son. In the dream, I knew we would have to move before he started high school. End of dream. We talked about the dream and agreed to move, giving us only two years to plan. We found a place in a different city and everything worked out fine. This is a great example of a warning inside of a directional dream.

Direction dreams are normally very clear. These dreams are a big picture overview of the plan we have for your lives. They are always bringing advanced notice to us to prepare us for the next assignment or move. In my dream, I was moving to a different city. I knew in the dream that my job was coming to an end and that I was going to be offered a job with better pay in a city closer to my family. End of dream. The next day I woke up thinking that was a weird dream. I loved my job and we were doing great there, but deep down inside I knew something was going to happen. Sure enough six months later I was notified of changes at work and my job was going to be cut. This is a typical direction dream, very simple, clear and way in advance. The colors should be bright and the emotions in the dream should be happy or excited for the adventure that awaits you.

List out the elements below that you can identify that are directional and what are the lessons provided.

_____

_____

_____

_____

_____

Warning Dreams:

Here is an example of a warning dream. List out the elements in the dream that you can identify that warn. What are the lessons provided?

Muted color or no color = These muted colors or lack of colors give you a sense of danger telling you you're going the wrong way. These dreams are about the battle for your destiny - divine purpose.

In the dream, you are driving your car and get a flat tire. You get out of the car and look for the tools and spare tire and get to work. The metaphor is this: this inconvenience is giving you time to think about where your life is headed. Your car represents your gifts, talents and abilities. It is a conversation starter keeping you from getting too far off track. Normally this is when your assignment has changed and you haven't received revelation or you were unable to hear it.

Where are you going? Why?

_____

_____

_____

List out the elements in the dream that you can identify that warn. What are the lessons provided?

_____

_____

_____

Instruction Dreams:

Bright or normal colors: these colors will vary depending on the amount of instructions needed for you to stay going in the right direction. Instruction dreams are like notes left on your pillow in the morning. They seem to be written with disappearing ink and they are easily forgotten if you don't write them down. A lot of time the instructions are concealed in our dreams and we need to learn how to find them and apply them to our lives. These types of dreams can save us so much time, energy and money if we just pay attention to them and apply them to our lives.

Here is an example of an instructional dream. List out the elements and the steps. What are the lessons provided?

Okay so let's look at an instruction dream metaphor. I had a dream of a big wave coming at me and I was told to go under and hold my breath for 10 seconds. I knew if I did this the wave would be over and I could come up for air and make it out okay.

_____

_____

_____

Wave Dreams:

When you see the wave and it's very close, coming right at you, it's normally in the next few days. If you see the wave in the distance, there is time to prepare for what's coming in the next couple of weeks. These dreams come to give you a warning so that you can respond well when the event happens. Normally it is work or family issues that seem overwhelming, but you will get through it.

List out the elements and the steps. What are the lessons provided?

_____

_____

_____

The number 10 is testing, so this was going to be a big test - a big wave and the number ten. However, if we look closely at the dream, we realize that if we hold our breath for 10 seconds, everything would be okay, the wave would be over. We would come up for air. Everything is fine. Think about this if you are holding your breath underwater are you able to speak? Of course not. What the dream is telling you is to not to respond to what's about to happen. As the dream played out, it was a coworker who was way out of line and tried to start something, and my job was not to respond. I decided to say a few things to defend myself. This was definitely not a good idea. I should have stayed silent and everything would have been way better.

This is the typical instruction dream, very metaphorical, and you have to figure out the language the vehicle that your dream is being presented to you in, so that you can do very well with these instructions.

List out the elements and the steps. What are the lessons provided?

_____

_____

_____

Flashback Dreams:

Flashback dreams are definitely related to instructional types of dreams. They are different in that you have a sealed message that you cannot open until it is time! And very often it is in real time. These types of dreams can be in the whole color spectrum from vivid color to black and white. The theme of the dream and what is being shown or told to you will determine what color palette you will dream in. This will take some time to develop a color code for flashback dreams.

Here is a flashback dream. List out the elements that take you back to the past or remind you of something former. What is the lesson provided?

_____

_____

_____

Okay so in this dream you are waiting to sign mortgage papers. You are waiting for the escrow officer to show up so that you can sign the deed to your new house. You walk into the room and sit down. The paperwork is in front of you and you remember that you have been here before. You begin to feel a bit uneasy and it becomes clear that something doesn't seem right. This is when you ask to step outside for five minutes so that you can think about this. The fragments of the dream should come back to you at this time. Ask yourself, "is there something I overlooked? Are the numbers right? Is this what I agreed to?" This can happen when you are purchasing a car, as well. Process through your emotions and make a decision.

_____

_____

_____

Look for Outliers

Outliers are dreams that don't fit in the healthy lens of your dream life. An outlier doesn't mean it is a lie. The personal exploration is to see if you are a contributing member of the origin of these dreams. This should bring you on a healthy pursuit to resolve the foundations of these dreams. Sometimes, outlier dreams have no bases and should be discarded.

In the categories below, identify what percentage of your dreams come from each one. You do not need to achieve 100%. Any percentage is very helpful to know and indicate.

Immoral thoughts, feelings, and actions:

Any dream that promotes thoughts, emotions, or actions that break away from your convictions, morals, and ideals would be an outlier.

_____%

Sexualized dreams:

Any dream that is sexualized that does not provide you with life-giving thoughts and feelings that establish and build your covenants, commitments, and marriage should be evaluated.

_____%

Feelings that go against what you believe:

These are dreams where you are breaking laws, breaking your faith, or going out of your way to harm others.

_____%

Past traumas:

When past traumas replay themselves in different ways in our dreams, we often see several variations of the same thing.

_____%

Hypothetical fears (what if dreams):

Monumental fears leading to dreams can be outliers kept in check. Examples of this would be simple fears exacerbated into life-altering outcomes.

_____%

Garbage Pizza dreams:

You watch an action movie and then have a dream that night about being in an action movie scene, and you are trying to escape the same plot.

_____%

Evaluate any assigned percentage of dreams that you have in the outlier category. If you placed a number on any one of these categories that is significant you have more self development, healing, and processing to do. Don't be ashamed, or be down about this. This is very exciting news that you have a clear area of opportunity that you can direct your focus on. *If you are having garbage pizza dreams then you are possibly exposing yourself to conflicting noise from your heart, mind or spirit. If your conscious is needing a certain frequency based on your values and beliefs and you feed it some garbage you may end up with garbage dreams.

Test your dream

Sometimes we get outlier dreams. Dreams that do not fit in our ideal dream lens. How do you know? We know if the dream we just had fits into our lens because we test it against our values, principles and purpose.

Write out a recent dream and test it. If the dream fits, define why it fits. If it doesn't fit then also define why.

_____

_____

_____

Now let's test the dream against these helpful questions.

_____

_____

1. Does the dream fit into my divine purpose today or down the road?

_____

_____

_____

2. Does the dream help me and or my family?

_____

_____

_____

3. Does the dream help my thoughts, emotions, and actions?

_____

_____

_____

4. Does the dream help me work through parts of my past?

_____

_____

_____

5.Does the dream have redemptive values I can gain from it?

_____

_____

_____

6. Does the dream help me materially today or in the foreseeable future?

_____

_____

_____

7. Does the dream break any commitments or covenants I currently have?

_____

_____

_____

8. Does the dream align with who I am and the other dreams I have?

_____

_____

_____

It is done

Ask yourself these questions to see if you have passed the dream test for outlier dreams.

Do you feel you have a clear release from the conditions of the dream? _____

Do you feel personal conviction anymore about the contents of the dream? _____

Do you feel you have moved on from the dream and its nature? _____

Do you feel the dream was an isolated experience and it has no footing in you?_____
If not, then you have your work cut out for you.

Timeline

If you were to list out your dreams on a timeline then they would be all connected. Of course, you will have outlier dreams that don't fit in the timeline. It's important to create those distinctions and understand when you have a dream that fits into the relational timeline of your life and when you have dreams that do not. For a simple visual exercise, number five dreams that come to mind using a simple phrase.

1._____

2. _____

3._____

4._____

5._____

Now place those numbers on a horizontal line in the order that you received them.

This is a visual of the chronological progression of your dreams. If you were to close this horizontal line it would become a circle. You are placed in the center of the circle. You are the dreamer and because you will always be at the center, your dreams will always have similar themes since you are involved.

Understanding the relational process of your dreams

The origin of a dream speaks directly to its author. You are the author of your dreams whether they are garbage pizza or of divine origin. You alone author your dreams. Your neighbor or your spouse do not alter your dreams. Once we realize this we embrace the relational process of dreaming.

The people in your dreams are an extension of your relationships.

List out the most common and familiar people in your dreams.

_____

_____

_____

Do you notice how they are all connected to you in some way? Perhaps they are an active person who is in a relationship with you on a daily basis or it is someone whom you visualize or think about often?

What are some common themes that are an extension of you that show up in your dreams?

_____

_____

_____

Do you notice how they are all connected to you in some way? These themes are not necessarily the themes of your neighbor. These are your themes and this understanding is the first phase in realizing the dreams are part of a relational process in which you author.

True or False

In our dreams truth and lies are relative to the dream. Many people are confused about whether something is true or false. Truth or the sense of truth is an extension of the dream. If you are looking for a literal interpretation then factual is what you have. 98% of your dreams will not have a literal interpretation. If your dream is signified or symbolic in nature then the truth that is found within your dream may not have the same factual magnitude as it does in your real life. You are learning a dream language and images are used to convey that language to you. This is a different language than the one you learned when you were awake.

Here is an example of relative truth:

Susie is sleeping next to a bear in her dream. Fight the urge to make this dream literal. It is true that Susie had this dream. She did have a dream sleeping next to a bear. This was a real dream. However, the bear in her dream was not equivalent to a literal bear in real life. It was a metaphorical or a symbolic bear. Are you able to distinguish the gray areas of "truth"?

Susie has a dream with five extra children in it. Fight the urge to make this dream literal. It is true that Susie had this dream. She did, in fact, have a dream about five kids. That is true. This was a real dream. However, the five children in her dream were metaphorical and symbolic in nature. This is not a false dream.

Can you say that a dream is true or false? Not in the general sense. Dreams are neutral. They only convey things that compel us to believe in the conveyed narrative, which we would then interpret to be accurate or not. Most of the implied meaning comes from our assumption of whether or not it's literal. If we can refrain from making our dreams literal for the large part, then we can begin to interpret its implied meaning.

You have a dream where you are sleeping next to a bear. Is it real?

_____

_____

_____

Is the bear actually a literal bear?

_____

_____

_____

Is the dream true or false?

_____

_____

_____

Your answer should be neither. The dream is not seeking a true or a false answer. Neither should you.

CHAPTER 5

CONTEXT AND CATEGORIES

Dreams should be evaluated over a continuum of one's life and in the totality of the dream itself. We as individuals should be mindful that our dreams are all connected in some way, even if we are the connection point. Outlier dreams are always a possibility, but not the norm. When we approach the interpretation of our dreams, we should keep in mind the previous dreams that we have had. What themes, understanding, and lessons are carried over? More than likely, we will see a progression of themes and a seasonal approach to the dreams we have.

Each dream we have is a whole unit. It would be silly and ridiculous to cut the dream in half and only evaluate one half of the dream. Furthermore, it would be equally nonproductive to only pick and choose parts of the dream that are more desirable to evaluate. The dream is a package; all contents should be evaluated equally, until experience leads us to discard them. If we can keep the unity of our dreams alive, then we will have greater success in understanding them. So make yourself a promise not to pick and choose in your dreams. Keep it together, and you will be much better off that way.

See, you have a dream and it has many parts to it. It would be inappropriate for you to grab one element of that dream and evaluate it as the whole of the entire dream. That element needs to be held in the tension of the preceding facts and the facts that come after. That is what we call context. We don't want to take sound bites out of our dream and make them sound like something they did not intend to say. We want them to be true to form and deliver the whole message that was originally intended. If there's an element in our dream that we don't like, we need to keep it right where it is so that we fully understand the context of our dreams.

Through line

If there was a string that went all the way through your dream what would it be?

_____

_____

_____

Here's an example of a dream. indicate the common thread that carries the entire dream?

I dreamed that I was sitting on a plane waiting to take off. I was waiting for my friend to join me hoping that he wouldn't miss the flight. There was another plane in front of the one that I was in waiting for the right conditions to take off. Finally, my friend that I was waiting for pulled up but he had fallen asleep in the car on the way to the airport and the driver was trying to wake him up. Then suddenly the other plane took off! I was so excited because we were the next flight out.

In this dream, the dreamer is definitely the focus. The whole dream is the dreamer's POV. They are waiting and watching all this happen right in front of their eyes. It is interesting how many things are in the way of their flight taking off on time, or if their friend will make it. This dream is about their life and how things beyond their control are hindering them from taking off into their destiny. Remember the rule: find yourself in the dream because 90% of the time you are the focus. The dream was given to you and for you.

Now it is your turn. Think about your most recent dream and indicate the common thread that is present in the beginning, middle and end of your dream. The common thread does not need to be profound. It can be a simple understanding or a perspective. Sometimes our dreams have a very visible cadence and sometimes they have an implied cadence.

_____

_____

_____

Stay true to your interpretation

When interpreting your dream you are analyzing the components of the dream to understand their nature and what they are trying to convey. You spot a theme, a vehicle, a type of dream that speaks to you as a method of interpretation. Perhaps your dream is signified and defined with caricatures. How will you begin to interpret this dream? Well, you have to go in the door that is presented to you within the dream. If the dream is symbolic then there will be icons for you to open. If you are in the middle of interpreting a signified or symbolic dream you are not allowed to switch styles of interpretation and make parts of your dream literal. You would be breaking the laws of interpretation, and you will be confused about the meaning of your dreams.

Here's an example of staying true to your interpretation:

Dream: A lady on a red bike driving, it into the ocean and it starts floating, then she starts flying.

Interpretation: This dream is about the dreamer. They will be on a passionate journey into some uncharted territory but they will make it through the uncertainty. Not only will they make it they will begin to soar above their original vision and goals.

Here is an example of not staying true to your interpretation:

Dream: A lady on a red bike driving it into the ocean and it starts floating, then she starts flying.

Interpretation: The lady is 50% the dreamer and 50% the neighbor who looks like the lady. The red bike is a real bike in the garage that she needs to ride into the ocean, and it's a symbolic bike that is about an idea the dreamer had. The dreamer must move next to the ocean to make her dream happen. The dreamer needs to enroll in flying lessons to make her dreams come true. The dreamer is failing at life because they are on a small red bike and not a car, and their favorite colors are blue and orange.

Identify how the dream was not interpreted correctly. What did the interpreter get wrong?

_____

_____

_____

Build out your personalized dream language

When you are dreaming, you are dreaming utilizing a personalized dream language. If you have not yet decided what language you would like to use then one will be implied to you. This is much harder to understand if you are not in agreement with designing your dream language. It is up to you to define the language in which your dreams are communicating to you. When you see a house, what do you believe about the house? When you see the mailman, what do you believe about the mailman? When you see food missing from your plate, what do you believe about that? Answer the above questions in addition to listing out 25 things, people, places, and objects that you are to self-define. What do you believe about each one?

_____

_____

_____

_____

_____

_____

_____

_____

Let's set up a few new personalized symbols. It will be an easy exercise.

What are three things you think of when you see a tornado?

_____

_____

_____

What are three feelings you produce when you see a candle?

_____

_____

_____

What are three memories you have when you see a cloud?

_____

_____

_____

What are three pictures you produce in your mind when you think of happiness?

_____

_____

_____

Categories in Dreams

Categories in dreams are very helpful when you're just starting off. A very large majority of authors and interpreters of dreams will convey a great emphasis on the categorical nature of dreams. It's important to be able to categorize your dreams. There are different kinds of people in your life and it's good to know when you're having dreams about your friends. Many dreams convey numbers and number sequences. It's also helpful to know when you have dreams about your hometown versus when you have dreams about traveling.

If you are to learn anything about dreams in this book, please do not deduce your dreams down to a category in which you overanalyze and overinspect. The categories in your dream are to highlight a greater purpose and a greater meaning outside of categorization. There are many who get excited to interpret their dreams, and they fall in love with dream dictionaries rather than the actual meaning of their dreams. Please shy away from dictionaries. Your dream language is specific to you, not to the dictionary.

Write out a few categories that you find is a common theme within your dreams.

_____

_____

_____

What colors are conveyed in your dreams?

_____

_____

_____

What kinds of people are conveyed in your dreams?

_____

_____

_____

What are common numbers conveyed in your dreams?

_____

_____

_____

What kind of weather is conveyed in your dreams?

_____

_____

_____

What is your relation to time in dreams?

_____

_____

_____

What kind of environments do you find yourself in inside of your dreams?

_____

_____

_____

CHAPTER 6

APPLICATION

Breaking down your dreams and reducing them to the simplest form: What is the dream saying? We do this by finding the focus of the dream. What is the critical element in the dream that if you took it away, there would be no more dream? That is what we are looking for.

When you look at your dreams, 90% of the time you will find that you are the focus. You need to find yourself in the dream. What are you doing? Saying? How are you participating?

Remember there's only one focus. The rest of the dream is either opportunities, promises and invitations or obstacles, issues and problems. Things that you need to walk into or things you are going to have to overcome. Looking at your dreams this way is the best way to understand them.

Below are some examples of dreams and what they mean.

Dream life process

Context of your life. How does this dream fit your life (i.e., education, training, desires, abilities, aptitude)?

The process of interpretation is determined relationally! Your symbols and stories are tailor-made for you. Your dreams are in a language that is unique to you.

Application

The dream is only the beginning of the invitation for you to change, believe, move, and grow into who you are intended to be.

Dream Exercise #1

I dreamed someone was trying to force their way into my car. I was in my car when it happened. They opened the door and were trying to get in. I was pushing them out. After a bit of a struggle, I got them out. End of dream

The dreamer is the focus.

Remember your car represents your gifts, talents and abilities. When you're in your car this is symbolic of your job. This is an attack on you personally, who you are, and what you do! This person is trying to take your job or harass you. The purpose of this type of dream is to prepare you for what's coming. This type of warning is very important to pay close attention to. You need to stay calm during this power struggle and don't say anything that you will regret. Everything will be okay if you don't lose your temper. Be ready for a test of your patience. Now if it's something trying to come in your car and you're not sure if it's human or not, this is a spiritual attack on you! And it's going to come after your mind and your emotions. The same thing applies. Stay at peace and respond appropriately.

Dream Exercise #2

Telescope dream

In my dream, I'm looking through a telescope towards the east. I currently live on the west coast and have no plans to move away, but in the dream I have a sense that I'm going to be moving east. End of dream.

In this dream the dreamer is the focus.

The context of the dreamer's life at the time of the dream doesn't make sense. This is a destiny dream. These dreams will be telling you of things to come and where you will live. The big clue is the dreamer is looking through a telescope! The metaphor is you are seeing into the far off future. The dreamer had a sense or feeling of something calling the into a distant land.

The most important thing you can do with this type of dream is to write it down and keep it in a safe place in a separate folder. Destiny dreams will leave an imprint on your mind and be with you throughout your life. By the way, some 15 years later the dreamer did move out of state towards the east to fulfill a big part of their life's calling.

Dream Exercise #3

I dreamed that I had a big hand in my car. I didn't even realize that I had it. I was getting something out of my car and it just automatically appeared. I began to laugh about it because it was so big. I got out of the car to show my friends. I woke up very excited!

The dreamer is the focus of this dream.

The context is the dreamer has something they need already, but they don't know it! In fact, they are surprised by this. Remember, your car represents your gifts, talents, and abilities. This dream implies that the dreamer has some hidden talent that's really going to help them. The metaphor of the hand could be understood a couple of ways: the hand that you're dealt in life. This dreamer was given a big hand, more than enough to do what they're called to do. Or we could look at it as a helping hand to help them accomplish their destiny. Either way, it's an awesome dream. The other thing to notice is that the hand just automatically appeared to them. This part of the dream implies that this gift will be hidden until its time. Then everything changes. The dreamer is laughing and showing their friends. This is a very exciting time in their life.

Dream Exercise #4

In this dream the dreamer is walking through a house. They know it's their house, but they have never been there or seen it before. As they walk through the house they come to the living room and it has a very big window. They walk over and look out of the window and see buildings and people. The dreamer then wakes up feeling refreshed and full of hope wondering about the dream.

The dreamer is the focus.

Okay, so the dreamer is walking through a house that they know is theirs, but they haven't seen it or been there before. This is speaking of the future and where they are headed. In this type of dream, you will want to ask yourself, "Do I like this house because this is where the trajectory of my life is taking me?" As the dreamer is walking through the house they are drawn to the window and they see a vision. Most of the time when you are looking out of a window in a dream you are having or seeing a vision. This type of vision is different from a night vision. A window vision is an invitation to participate with God to bring it into reality / into this world. There is a big difference between the two. A night vision is literally how things you see will happen. You don't have to participate for them to come to pass. In the dream, the images they saw were places they would go, things they would build, and people that they would impact. It's a great dream revealing things of the future and what their life would be like. If you like what you see, keep heading in the same direction! If not, make some changes and move forward and keep on dreaming.

Dream Exercise #5

I dreamed that I came to the end of the road and I was going to have to make a turn. The choice was to turn right or left. When I stopped, I noticed that I had crossed the line so I had to back up and get behind the line. I noticed that two cops were watching me. I decided to make a left turn and started to drive down the road. I had a great feeling that something very good was going to happen.

The dreamer is the focus.

In this dream, they are driving and all of a sudden the road ends. They only have two choices: turn right or turn left. They can't go back to what was. Everything changes. Suddenly, their life is headed in a different direction. Everything begins again. Think of it as the beginning of a new season in your life.

Here are some of the signs of entering a new season;

You will find yourself lacking vision for the future. Intuitively you will feel like you should turn around and go back the other way, because it feels like the job you have or journey you're on is a dead end. Remember, during this time you can't see where you're going. All you can see is a macro vision of what's right in front of you. Seeing every detail can be very distracting, causing anxiety, fear of failure, or feeling a lack of purpose. But wait, just wait. This is the place where we meet God… hold on… this is when the new normal comes! This is where your dreams come true! It's the end of a chapter and the beginning of a new one! Keep moving forward! And get ready, your vision will come back! Everything around you will have changed. You're now in a new season! You will notice a new passion for life and what you're created to do. It will take some time for your vision to adjust to where you're going, but keep looking forward until you get your focus back. Then you will see clearly what's in front of you, and all the changes around you as you enter into the new season full of hope for what the future will bring.

The two cops were there to protect this transition so we didn't try to keep going in the same direction.

Now it's your turn. Let's follow the steps in this book and break down your dreams into the simplest form.

Dream life process

Context of your life. How does this dream fit your life (i.e., education, training, desires, abilities, aptitude)?

The process of interpretation is determined relationally! Your symbols and stories are tailor-made for you. Your dreams are in a language that is unique to you.

Application

The dream is only the beginning of the invitation for you to change, believe, move, and grow into who you are intended to be.

Your Dream Exercise #1 _____

_____

_____

Your Dream Exercise #2 _____

_____

_____

Your Dream Exercise #3 _____

_____

_____

Your Dream Exercise #4 _____

_____

_____

Your Dream Exercise #5 _____

_____

_____

CHAPTER 7

DESTINATION

Finding the top ten dreams of your life

After meeting with thousands of people regarding their dreams, I like to take people on a journey of the top 10 dreams of their life. It's a straightforward exercise, but a profound one. The first thing I instruct them to do is to write down the ten dreams that stand out as the most profound. For some people, this may be a simple exercise. But for others, this could be quite challenging. That's okay. Do what you can.

These dreams are profound because they either stick out as completely different, or there is a prevalent element within the dream that makes it profound to us. The dream's profound nature is essential and key to unlocking its origin and direction. If you see any areas of opportunity within those profound dreams, perhaps things you know you are working on or things you experienced in your life, then that would be time for inner healing. If those profound dreams take you into places in the future that you have never considered before, then contemplate those dreams. Embrace those dreams and pursue them.

Take your time and write out the top ten dreams of your life. Once you have written them down, compare them, contrast them, find the thread, find the theme, see the sequence, and see the journey in which you are being led by your dreams through life.

1._____

2._____

3._____

Make a symbol of each dream and place it in these puzzle pieces.

Each piece is a puzzle piece of you.

Time to Record

Every dream you have is worthy of being recorded. Utilize a simple method.

Journaling and Track Your Dreams

Write down the dream and the date.

_____

_____

Write down the interpretation.

_____

_____

Write down what you think will happen and how it will apply to your life.

_____

_____

Then, once the dream is fulfilled:

Write down what happened and how it was fulfilled.

_____

_____

Write down how you were right and where you were wrong.

_____

_____

Thank you so much for going through the Dream Workbook! Keep dreaming!